£8·95

WAST
WI DA
VALKYRIES

... fale & walked down
to the shore in the
sunshine. Foula lay
clear & still like an
uncut jewel against an
...

CHRISTINE DE LUCA

WAST
WI DA
VALKYRIES

Poems in English and Shetland Dialect

THE SHETLAND LIBRARY

BY THE SAME AUTHOR

Voes & Sounds, *The Shetland Library 1994*

ISBN 0 904562 64 6

Published by The Shetland Library, Lerwick, 1997

Printed by Shetland Litho, Lerwick

a peerie mindin on
my midder an faider

Jemima Jamieson Halcrow (1910-1982)

an

Alexander Pearson (1913-1991)

Trowe wir minds wir ain aald language
still keeps rinnin laek a tön;
Laek da laverik ida hömin,
sheerlin whin da day is döne;
Laek da seich o wind trowe coarn
at da risin o da mön.

from "A Skyinbow o Tammy's"
by Vagaland

ACKNOWLEDGMENTS

Some of the poems in this collection have appeared in the following:

JOURNALS AND BROADSHEETS: Lines Review, Skinklin Star, The New Shetlander

ANTHOLOGIES: The Ice Horses (2nd Shore Poets' Anthology) Scottish Cultural Press 1996; Mindin Rhoda, Shetland Folk Society 1995; Norman MacCaig A Celebration, Chapman 1995.

ARTICLES: "Landscapes, Lives and Literature" in the 1996 Journal of the Scottish Association of Geography Teachers; The Herald

RADIO: Some of the dialect poems have also been broadcast on Radio Scotland and Radio Shetland.

POETRY & ART: "Present Poets" (National Museums of Scotland).

Grateful acknowledgment is given to all who have encouraged this collection in this way.

The author would also like to thank the following individuals and organisations:

The Shetland Library for financing this collection, and in particular, John Hunter (Chief Librarian) for his support.

John and Lawrence Graham, editors of the New Shetlander and nourishers of the dialect.

Pat Robertson for permission to quote from her husband's poem "A Skyinbow o Tammy's."

Tessa Ransford and members of the School of Poets, Edinburgh, for continued encouragement and criticism.

Alexa Rutherford, for her art work

Book designed by Alan Victor ASTD of Court Graphic Design, Edinburgh

CONTENTS

Survival tactics

Poems for bairns

Alzheimer sequence

Postscript

FOREWORD

Christine De Luca's 'Voes and Sounds' earned her the
Shetland Literary prize in 1996. I have no doubt that this,
her second collection of poems, will be a future contender.

Once again it has been a privilege to assist Christine in
bringing this collection to print. Enjoy reading her poems
with the same pleasure as I have had in publishing them.

J.G. HUNTER A.L.A.
Chief Librarian

Wast owre

Dark burn ta voe, a rinkel
bi Nederdale, trist slow slockit
in a sea-balled ayre . . .

Fae da *Green Holm* scarfs arrow low
mallies bank stiffly troo sea furrows.

Papa, *priest isle*: dere's nane ta lay
haands on ta sain noo.

Linga, *hedder isle*: a sea hairst:
piltocks, whelks, selkies, waar.

Hildis isle: tree score o sels neebin
slidder ta safety in Tangi Voe.

Da Shingies: *rocks in sun* at spills gowld.
Tirricks faest, dive low an wild.

Da sels is gien ta Hildasay da day.
Oksna: silent *seal isle*.

---

scarfs: *shags*; mallies: *fulmers*; troo: *through*; ta sain: *to bless*; hedder: *heather*; piltocks: *saithe*; waar: *seaweed*; tree: *three*; neebin: *dozing*; slidder: *slither*; tirricks: *arctic terns*; sels, selkies: *seals*; da day: *today*.

Mirknen haps a rummelled broch on Houlland's knowe,
rowes hit in a twilt o lavendar: saft smored as a Danish Hjøllund
a year ago. Da line o da prow is sib an da soonds on da tongue
but dis laand canna scoarn da forest, fat byres an grit rigs o coarn.
Here hit's a tooder o hedder an da mintiest flooers. Fae da broch
da wastside raiks aa aroond: Aid Voe spörs ta da nort; bi wast
a headicraa ta Burrafirt, ta Foula an Waas. Soothbye, a vire o voes
at Sandsoond an Skeld - Skjáldr o da sagas. A year is come
richt roond. I da simmir dim, sungaets, we mark da rim
o da broch-time circles: walk da mairches o a twalmont gien.

---

mirknen: *twilight*; haps: *wraps in shawl*; rummelled: *collapsed*; rowes: *wraps*; twilt: *quilt*;
smored: *suffocated, drowned*; da: *the*; sib: *related*; scoarn: *imitate*; grit: *large*; tooder:
tousle; mintiest: *tiniest*; raiks: *roves*; spörs: *enquires, with a proposal in mind*; headicraa:
somersault; vire: *a great beauty*; sungaets: *clockwise*; twalmont: *a year*.

Wasterwick

Wasterwick, auld wife o da sea, worn
tae a beauty only age can bring. Du sits
straight-backed, airms reck oot
bi clett an stack. Dy sang is
da sang o sels an a thoosand shiftin shalls
is dey beach demsels. Da Waarie Gyo
is a secret fowld i dy skurt, whaar
a kittle o tang swills to an fro.

Du gies hooseroom tae a swap o scarfs,
lodgins ta mallies. A shjalder swanks
apö dy shooder, nest safe in a reffel
o trefoil an smora. Banks-flooers
mak a wavy aedge ta dy simmer hap.

We look on dee at's cradled grown men,
trace lines o kennin on dy wise repose.
Da wasterin sun at faas saaftly lays
a wild rose apo dy granite face.

---

da: *the*; clett: *cliff, rock, crag*; stack: *column of rock in the sea*; dy: *your (familiar)*; shalls: *shells*; dey: *they*; demsels: *themselves*; gyo: *steep, narrow inlet*; fowld: *fold*; i: *in*; skurt: *bosom*; kittle: *tickle*; tang: *seaweed*; du: *you (familiar)*; gies: *gives*; tae, ta: *to*; swap: *a sudden beat or blow*; scarfs: *shags*; mallies: *fulmers*; shjalder: *oyster catcher*; apö: *on*; shooder: *shoulder*; reffel: *tangle*; smora: *clover*; banks flooers: *sea pinks*; aedge: *edge*; hap: *shawl*; dee: *you (familiar)*; at's: *who has*; kennin: *knowing*; faas: *falls*; saaftly: *softly*.

Herrin days, Waas, c 1890

Waas, Vágr,
variorum o voes an soonds:
rare lie o laand.

Herrin boats tack oot bi Linga
fae lea ta ocean dunt.
Names ta strange at -
Myrtle, Wild Rose, Violet -
dark petals on a simmer wind.

Men harned ta varg shut nets
is hömin darkens; drift
waakrife ta Foula; rise
i da hert-holl o da nicht
ta heave an haul, shack oot
da spricklin siller.
On every boat, a boy,
saft haands sweein
wi da cooch an saat, coils
sabbin bush ropes.

Russet sails rise
ta tize da wind
an, i da dimriv, stream
back in da Wastern Soond:
Myrtle, Wild Rose, Violet.

Six i da mornin,
shore huts spunder tae anidder day.
Da hidmost creel is swung ashore.
Coopers gadder, gutters claag,
da smiddy clangs. Aroond da voe,
fae Pointataing ta Saatness
maas callyshang,

sic a hooro, is women bend
owre haepit troughs:
gut an pack, gut an pack,
tu'pence an hour; saat dem doon
afore da mirknen, afore
anidder shoal slidders fae a creel,

afore steam dowes da petals
o da Myrtle, Wild Rose, Violet,
an laeves an empty pier.

Vágr: *Norse name for Waas (Walls)*; variorum: *decoration*; voes: *long sea inlets*; soonds: *sounds*; dunt: *heavy blow, bump*; to strange: *to wonder, marvel*; harned: *hardened*; varg: *messy work*; shut: *shoot*; hömin: *twilight*; waakrife: *sleepless*; da: *the*; hert-holl: *the very centre, middle*; spricklin: *wriggling*; siller: *silver (herrings)*; swein: *stinging*; cooch: *tar*; saat: *salt*; bush ropes: *heavy ropes to weight the bottom of the nets*; tize: *entice*; dimriv: *dawn*; spunder: *race*; tae: *to*; anidder: *another*; hidmost: *last*; gadder: *gather*; claag: *speak noisily*; smiddy: *forge*; maas: *seagulls*; callyshang: *(from noun) noisy dispute*; sic: *such*; hooro: *uproar*; haepit: *heaped*; dem: *them*; mirknen: *darkness*; slidders: *slithers*; dowes: *fades*.

5

Dark burn ta voe, a rinkel
bi Nederdale, trist slow slockit
in a sea-baaled ayre. At da beach
o Dale, noosts gaan at Foula, turn
vod een ta her shaalds. Fae Muness
shö's held in an artist's haand:
Valhalla, veiled paradise, built
lik a saga ta swall ta her heichts
wi every seein, every tellin. Winjanes
means whit hit's aye meant:
headland fur pasture. Ponies
startle dere, tak ta da hill.
Der manes lift lik a dizzen Valkyries
fleein da battle. Laand an sea
is still a skirmish. Unawaar,
selkies rowl i da laebrack,
bask safely on Sel Ayre.
An kittiwakes cruise: effortless
rollerbladers o da banks.
Da erne at eence ruled dem
is lang gien fae his stack.
Every sea bicht riven
fae Dale ta Deep Dale
has jaws risped wi yackles.

Time is mizzered here
bi da sea's favours: a tirse
o takkin, grindin,
an endless beachin; but fur wis,
travaillers o da wastern aedge,
hit's a time ta tak, ta pick owre
gaets wir taen, or no taen,
on dis wir langest vaege.

wast: *west*; da: *the*; Valkyries: *Norse goddesses who conducted the slain from the battlefield to Valhalla*; ta: *to*; rinkel: *tinkling noise*; bi: *past, by*; trist: *thirst*; slockit: *slaked*; baaled: *thrown*; noosts: *beach hollows to shelter boats*; gaan: *gaze*; vod: *empty, unoccupied*; een: *eyes*; shaalds: *shallows (fishing grounds)*; shö: *she*; whit: *what*; hit: *it*; dere: *there*; der: *their*; dizzen: *dozen*; selkies, sels: *seals*; rowl: *roll*; i: *in*; laebrack: *surf*; banks: *sea cliffs*; erne: *sea eagle*; eence: *once*; dem: *them*; gien: *gone*; bicht: *bite*; riven: *torn*; aedged: *edged*; risped. *from noun risp, a rasp or file*; yackles: *molars*; mizzered: *measured*; tirse: *an agitation, temper*; takkin: *taking*; wis: *us*; travaillers: *walkers*; owre: *over*; gaets: *paths*; wir: *we have, our*; taen: *taken*; dis: *this*; vaege: *journey*.

Oot o scöl on winter days, we'd sprit
across da fud ta Lizzie Coutts' Knowe
sledges nyiggin at wir heels lik aaber whalps.

Hills wirna better med fur sledgin:
low enyoch fur a quick bassel tae da tap;
steep enyoch ta taste da aedge
o danger; lang enyoch ta savour.

We'd pile on
twartree o wis
een on tap o tidder:
belly-gutsie fur da brave
nae trace o faer.
Da runk o iron apö ice,
snaa spindrifts smookin
i da face. A rummel
o scriechs is we swooshed
owre every bump
afore we cummelled.

Dan hame fur tae, glivs ice-matted,
haands red raw wi pooin apo kiarr.
Inbye fae da spunder o da nicht
wi haet tiftin anunder wir nails
an wir een blinded i da licht.

---

scöl: *school*; sprit: *dash, race*; fud: *flat patches of fields at voe head*; nyggin: *tugging*; aaber: *eager*; whalps: *puppies*; wirna: *were not*; enyoch: *enough*; bassel: *struggle*; twartree: *two or three*; een: *one*; tidder: *the other*; belly-gutsie: *sledging face-downwards*; runk: *resounding rhythm*; apö: *on*; snaa: *snow*; spindrifts: *(sea) spray*; smookin: *suddenly covering*; rummel: *(from verb) to collapse*; scriechs: *screeches*; cummelled: *turned upside down*; tae: *high tea*; glivs: *gloves*; pooin: *pulling*; kiarr: *coir rope*; spunder: *(from verb) to race*; tiftin: *throbbing*; anunder: *under*; een: *eyes*.

A boannie nicht for castin kale:
a fat mön vaegin owre Sannis,
a hale gadderie o laads an lasses.

A spree i der blöd,
laads loupit dykes
purled kale-stocks
iggit een anidder on
ripe da rigs
hunse fur hens
whit a stramash
an dan da dash
tae a porch door
lift da sneck
ball in da booty
rin like da mellishon
dunna look back.

But dee an me
pooskered wi da bassel
fell ahint ta draa breath,
taste wir first smoorikin.
But aa I can mind is da mön
gaffin at me in mi cöttikins
wis ahint a uncan barn
an dy blate hansel
anunder a kendlin o starns.

hansel: *gift to mark an inaugural occasion;* castin kale: *the Hallowe'en tradition of stealing croft produce such as cabbages and throwing them in doorways;* mön: *moon;* vaegin: *wandering;* hale: *whole;* gadderie: *gathering;* spree: *jollification;* der: *their;* blöd: *blood;* loupit: *jumped;* purled: *poked about;* kale-stocks: *cabbages;* iggit on: *incited;* een anidder: *one another;* to ripe: *to harvest;* rigs: *fields;* hunse: *rummage;* stramash: *commotion;* dan: *then;* tae: *to;* sneck: *latch;* ball: *throw;* da mellishon: *the devil;* dunna: *do not;* dee: *you (familiar);* pooskered: *exhausted;* bassel: *struggle;* ahint: *behind;* draa: *draw;* wir: *our;* smoorikin: *kiss;* aa: *all;* mind: *remember;* gaffin: *laughing;* mi: *my;* cöttikins: *ankle socks;* wis: *us;* uncan: *unfamiliar;* dy: *your (familiar);* blate: *shy;* anunder: *under;* kendlin: *live coals;* starns: *stars.*

Busta, Sannis

Gyo o Busta, roond is a cockle: we'd watch
fur sels here, skip stons, kyemp fur da finest shalls.
We'd barely lift wir een ta see hits shape:
dat sam shall pattern at spread hitsel
owre midders' makkin: therteen loops taen in
dan löt oot slowly on an openwark o gengs:
waves at shaded ta inky-blueness wi da wind.

Da day, hoors swittle trowe dy fingers
is du seeks, as eence I sought, da perfect ston
ta skip. Tree skips'll dö, een mair is last year.
Da rings du maks spread fast. Last simmer here
eicht selkies bobbed lik bowes: eyed wis, dived,
eyed wis again. Dey left nae spreadin rings:
art hoidin artistry. I watch dy ston dance,

defy da wyes o watter, da skip o years.
Wi dee A'm richt back: we skile fur sels,
seek cockle shalls, weigh da import o stons;
skip an höve dem, fur da sea ta bring back,
ta lay up and mak again in time's lap.

---

da cockle shall: *a lace pattern in knitting (which requires 13 stitches to be purled together)*; gyo: *steep, narrow inlet*; sels, selkies: *seals*; kyemp: *compete*; shalls: *sea shells*; wir: *our*; een: *eyes*; hits: *its*; dat, that: at: *that, which*; hitsel: *itself*; midder: *mother*; makkin: *knitting*; loops: *stitches*; taen: *taken*; dan: *then*; löt: *let (past tense)*; openwark: *lace knitting*; gengs: *rows of knitting*; da day: *today*; hoors: *hours*; swittle: *splash gently*; trowe: *through*; dy: *your (familiar)*; du: *you (familiar)*; dö: *do*; een: *one*; is: *as, than*; maks: *makes, knits*; eicht: *eight*; bowes: *buoys*; wis: *us*; dey: *they*; hoidin: *hiding*; wyes: *ways*; dee: *you (familiar)*; skile: *look with eyes shielded*; höve: *throw*; dem: *them*; lay up: *cast on stitches*.

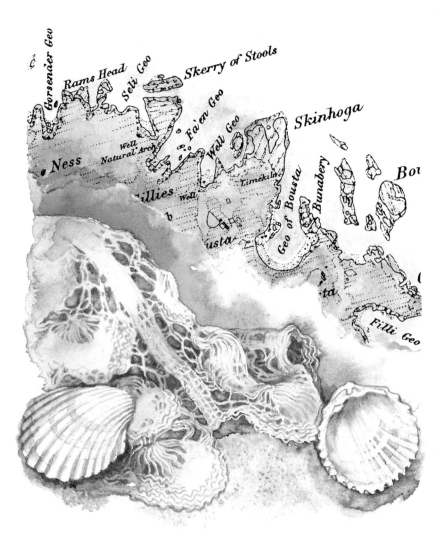

Idder erts

*The morning brings summer
suddenly, but no birdsong.*

A line of hills stretches from *Cnoc Mor* to *Sgurr Mor*:
Big Hill to Big Peak. Their names summon like bells:
Hill of the Cows, Hill of the Well, Hill of the River Mouth.

They are recumbent, wearied as old monsters,
their skins weathered, their breathing stilled.
Each has seen young Staffa's columns rear, and spill:
a soufflé stiffening in a crystal dish. They have seen
mountains lifted, lowered, ice ages come and go,
the machair tilt from the ocean slowly.
While they hunched their backs to the wind
sand re-arranged itself endlessly. They have seen

a living wrested from the soil, lazy beds turned, sickles curving
through the Cornfield of the Meadow, spades thrust
in the Hill of the Digging. They have felt the air cowled
with prayer, as monks shuddered past Martyrs' Bay.

These hills still catalogue the tramp of pilgrims,
less sure-footed, but faith rock-rooted,
following a circuitous and harder way.

Inchcolme Abbey

The Inchcolme ferry steers
through shipping lanes
across the tides of time
to this abrupt tranquillity.

An abbey raised squarely on a rock:
here windows of narrow lights were built;
and inner court with rows of hewn stone.

Four hundred years have passed
since bells rang round this tower;
since matins, lauds and vespers
linked the day in prayer: unbroken
centuries of supplication.
And still the chant is strong in stone
except the long sea wind has softened speech
and rounded edges. In every cloistered step
in nomine Domini quietly resounds.

In the garden eyes cower
from sharpened light,
senses turn corners
to the bright immediate.
Lush growth abounds unchecked.

Thou art all fair, my love,
thou art altogether lovely.

From each wild rose, heart petals fall:
a smudge on skin, a touch of limp
cool smoothness; ground strewn
with aromatic silences.

A garden enclosed
is a spring shut up,
a fountain sealed.

As sun lowers, symbol
upon symbol unfolds:
rose petals, stone,
old as the hills, old
as resilience, fragility.

(1 Kings 6 v36;   Song of Songs 4 v7 12 ; 5 v16)

Roond da wirld as peerie bairns
wis roond da rods o Bressa:
da kent wirld circumnavigated
in tricycles an prams. Takkin
Da Dunter roond Noss an Bressa
is still a vaege apön a wirld scale.
Aert history lockit up in rocks:
deserts rear as saandston banks.
Dey tell der tale: foo dey aedged
fae a tropic an her dulskit airms
tae an arctic skurt; foo shö wrat
her ticht history on dem wi wave
an wind an ice.

Swall lifts wis in a cave.
A stour o Eden's plankton shaas
in a blinkie's licht, an da green-
black sheen o scarfs. Ledged high,
dey dicht der wings, stretch dem
ta dry. Dey live da quiet life, yet
aye riggit for a foy.

Oot on da banks, a high-rise life:
up, up, ledge apö ledge o solan,
maalies, a mafia o swaabies.
A callyshang: fast maet
an faerdie-maet;
a constant harangue.

At da nort end o Bressa
a raft o dunters bobs; selkies wait
fur a silent tide ta turn.
Anidder history is bön written here:
o cleared laand, vod hooses, fat sheep;
o young men press-ganged.

But still dere's change: new hooses,
laand wrocht again. Bressa's
on da move, stane bi stane.

---

da: *the*; peerie: *little*; wis: *was, us*; rods: *roads*; vaege: *journey*; apön, apö: *on;* aert: *earth*;
lockit: *locked*; banks: *sea cliffs*; dey: *they*; der: *their*; foo: *how*; aedged: *edged*; dulskit:
sluggish, torpid; airms: *arms*; tae, ta: *to*; skurt: *bosom*; shö: *she*; wrat: *wrote*; dem: *them*;
swall: *sea swell*; stour: *dust*; shaas: *shows*; blinkie: *torch*; scarfs: *shags*; riggit· *dressed*; foy:
celebration; solan: *gannets*; maalies: *fulmers*; swaabies: *great black-backed gulls*; callyshang:
noisy dispute; maet: *food*; faerdie-maet: *food for a journey*; nort: *north*; dunters: *eider ducks*;
selkies: *seals*; anidder: *another*; is bön: *has been*; vod: *unoccupied*.

A constellation surprises the night sky, rises
behind tall skylines; abruptly transfigures
into a bridge spanning an incongruous sky.
Then it reveals itself - weight and counterweight -
the dark arm of a crane, lit with fairy lights.

As we journey three more cranes light
the night, parade above the west end.
Rakishly they decorate decay: cavalcade
toward a new year. By day, they destroy
the old order, lift out drabness, place
new cornerstones. But tonight, lit up,
they are three high crosses, making
a Calvary of Christmas, stabbing the skyline
with their over-arching goodwill.

It is April in Manhattan.
We pull collars up against sleet;
dodge steaming manholes,
the splash of taxis.

Street noises layer themselves:
the basal hum of traffic,
bassooning horns
the sharp yawn of sirens.

Occasional churches surprise
like aconites in winter.
They do not fit the squareness,
the right and leftedness.
But these shapes I recognise:
their scale, their odd small symmetry.
Bewilderment retreats
in complete silence;
in the cusp of windows
and in Easter flowers.

When night comes I shut out
the confines of tall streets, sleep
vertical between glass sheets.
I dream of birds which seek
footholds in ledgeless territory;
horizons in a Mondrian maze.
The morning brings summer
suddenly, but no birdsong.

Jutland, 1995

I can close my eyes now and see
bikes spin past stiff wheat,
past barley combed by a warm wind.
In the haze, wide-angled, can gaze
at cows in salt shallows, standing
dark against light-bleached land
as they have stood for centuries,
Cuyp or Vermeer-like.

And by a lake at Hampen,
the deep focus in the mind's eye
of wind on silk reeds
and the swither of dragonflies,
a surprise of blueness.

This landscape is primeval,
ancient, fluvio-glacial:
a shard of time defining space.

All evening the irrigation wheel pulses,
moves imperceptibly. Jets of water
parabola towards a moon, I remember,
sickled gold on lavender.

A hairst mön rose apo seed gadderers is dey purled
late ita saandy aert, willin wild girse ta growe tick.
Awaar o dem fae da forest, deer smootit inta mirknen.

Lik a hyook, shö hung high, is fock traipsed hame
clugs truckin rigs o stubble, laevin laand trig stookit.
Deer fled da scent o hirdin, an bere in wippit baands.

Whin da first horses booed tae da bend, a man wid set
da reaper's basque: maa da sweerie-geng. While deer
tipped tae a filsket mön, horses strained i der stall.

Dastreen, shö kyempit wi lichts fae a combine at glaeped
ten fit swaars at ee sitten. Twa deer shivered trowe da bere,
makkin hit ring is dey reeselled da hingin heads.

---

hairst: *harvest*; mön: *moon*; Hjøllund: *settlement in north central Jutland*; purled: *poked*;
aert: *soil*; girse: *grass*; tick: *thick*; dem: *them*; smootit: *moved furtively*; mirknen: *twilight*;
hyook: *sickle*; shö: *she*; fock: *folk*; traipsed: *wandered*; truckin: *trampling*; trig: *tidily*;
stookit: *set up in groups of sheaves*; da: *the*; hirdin: *harvest*; bere: *barley*; wippit: *twisted,
coiled*; baands: *straw used to bind sheaf*; booed: *bowed*; bend: *horse harness*; maa: *cut with
scythe*; sweerie-geng: *the first, and most difficult row in knitting*; tipped: *moved jauntily*;
filsket: *playful, frisky*; der: *their*; dastreen: *last night*; kyempit: *competed*; glaeped: *swal-
lowed greedily*; fit: *feet*; swaars: *swathes of grain*; ee: *one*; trowe: *through*; reeselled: *shook
vigorously*.

Harthope, Spring 1996

Today a buzzard has us in his sights.
On wide wings he tilts on updrafts;
hangs high, pretends disinterest.

The burn is a map of territories
dippers have defined. We disturb them
accidentally; set them on edge.

The valley makes no mask of history.
Here ice lumbered down from Cheviot,
left its mark, its wearied dumping.

Shrunk burns now shuffle in its place,
in garments made for their maturity;
equivocate by the season,
abandon channels, forge new ones.

Upstream an otter has left odour
on the biggest rock. A deep pool round it.
A red squirrel has dropped hazelnuts:
cups split from Spring's neat cabinet.

A fox has left the wishbone of the woodcock
quite intact: a fastidious skeleton dressed
to kill in three best feathers.

Spring has barely reached the crags.
Cheviot's white shoulder glistens
in the sun, too glacial for comfort.

Cold Law is sprung with a mattress
of faded heather. The air has a strong bite.
In sunless spots snow fingers melt
and freeze to a slush of lingering gems.

We pick our way: our footprints make
as little difference in the span of things
as puffs of pollen.

Tonight the fox and otter will be on the move:
patrol their marches. The stoat will shudder
at the buzzard's wing.

Lanzarote, 1994

We are old now. All these years
we scooped a living
from the slag of Timanfaya.
Each greening circle of black soil
a defiance against gravity,
against a constant wind:
it cauldroned from the hills by day
and in the evening simmered
off the sea.

That honeycomb of walls around our plots,
we built them, year on year, rebuilt
like worker bees. There are no boulders
that we did not lift a dozen times.
For fifty years we cleared
the ash of stones, until
we had the finest tilth in Tinajo.
Our grapes gave good wine,
plumped with the water that I carried
and a smudge of dew.

Now we sit at this café, quietly,
your weathered hands around a coke.
Tourists buzz brightly.
We are museum pieces.
In Sunday best, you are ill at ease,
shift in your seat.
We have no words to tease
out our life

to wrap it up.
It is an hour until the mass is said,
until the cup is raised.
Only the old wait for the mass now.

We will go back by bus.
I will shield my eyes from our fields, in case
stones have reclaimed their place.

(Vineyards in Lanzarote are pits of black ash soil, each vine
sheltered by a semi-circular wall.)

Idder fock

He wid see me is I roonded
da shooder o da Kloss,
lift his een, but keep his sye
i da rhythm o centuries.

aesy shair: *easy chair*; fock: *folk*; kyerried: *carried*; spack: *spoke*; da: *the*; waa: *wall*; abön: *above*; raep: *line or pole attached to mantelpiece*; twa: *two*; pictirs: *pictures*; paet reek: *peat smoke*; dey: *they*; atween: *between*; no: *not*; kennin: *knowing*; whit: *which*; wye: *way*; ta: *to*; fyaarmin: *fawning*; lauchin: *laughing*; swack: *active, energetic*; sheeld: *fellow*; wis: *was*; een: *eyes*; smeegin: *smirking*; anunder: *underneath*; grit: *large*; bummer: *bulky*; cep: *cap, hat*; pairt: *part*; prunk: *smart, poised*; apö: *on*; airm: *arm (of chair)*.

Aesy shair bi da stove,
Grandpa sat
while da women fock
fetched an kyerried
an spack.

On da waa, abön da raep,
twa muckle pictirs hung,
yallow wi paet reek: dey'd come
wi Capstan coupons
atween da wars.

   "Atween Twa Fires" indeed:
   da fine figure o a man, sittin
   at a table, no kennin whit wye
   ta turn; an twa women
   fyaarmin.

   An da silk sark an frills
   o *"Da Lauchin Cavalier"*.
   A swack sheeld he wis:
   black een smeegin at you
   fae anunder a grit bummer
   o a cep.

Grandpa played da pairt, while
prunk apö da airm, his cat sat
waitin for Franz Hals
ta tak his paints
an come back.

Auntie Baabie,
fowr generations pairtin wis,
an her paece, wir play.
Efter ninety year, nae muckle left
ta say?

Late i da mornin
twa black legs
at da tap o da laft ledder.
Smucks trivvelin doon peerie-wyes
nae budder.

Wöshed her
in water fae da burn;
redded her hair, slow ta da waist.
Curn black hit wis;
scored an plaited it,
wippit hit roond her lugs:
a lass at haert.

Bakit oat scones
klined dem fur wis
wi fresh weet butter; fed
da black fant o da stove, made maet.
Nivver dippit her:
nae saet.

On da heicht o da paet stack,
shö watched wir biggin: tapster,
keepin her counsel.
Straight mossy eens fur da waa,
a haert a blue clods:
nae bassel.

Last ta bed
shö slockit da lamp,
restit da stove
slow stramp.

Whin we left fur hame
sixpences i wir löfs shö birsed
an blissit wis
wi a wird.

---

fowr: *four*; wis: *us, was*; paece: *peace, silence*; wir: *our*; efter: *after*; nae muckle: *not much*; i: *in*; da: *the*; tap: *top*; laft: *loft*; ledder: *ladder*; smucks: *slippers*; trivvelin: *groping, feeling the way*; peerie-wyes: *gently*; budder: *bother*; wöshed: *washed*; redded: *combed*; ta: *to*; curn: *(the colour of) currants*; hit: *it*; wippit: *coiled*; lugs: *ears*; bakit: *baked*; klined: *spread*; dem: *them*; fresh (butter): *unsalted*; weet: *wet*; fant: *hunger*; maet: *food*; nivver: *never*; dippit: *sat down*; saet: *seat*; paet: *peat*; shö: *she*; biggin: *building*; tapster: *'top dog'*; eens: *ones*; waa: *(outside) wall (of peatstack)*; bassel: *struggle*; slockit: *extinguished*; restit: *banked*; stramp: *firm step*; löfs: *palms*; birsed: *pressed*; blissit: *blessed*; wird: *word*.

Whit is it aboot dis jug
at stricks at memory:
strippit broon lem,
a benkled lid,
nae special charm?
Yet I lift hit again
an drink psalms.

"Tak dis jug tae dy faider
i da yerd."
I'd carry hit an da biblical wirds
rowed in a cloot.

Dem at gowled is dey gud oot
carryin da seed
'll come back singin for joy
is dey bring in da shaeves.

Lookin back
hit wis pure *'Song o Songs'*:
up da Kloss o Voe, laevin
doon'oose: a mile hit felt lik
tryin no ta spill.

Dis is da time fur singin;
da sang o doos is i da rigs.

He wid see me is I roonded
da shooder o da Kloss,
lift his een, but keep his sye
i da rhythm o centuries.

Coarn fell in swaars o stoor.
I reeselled me wye, truckin
da ruckly strae, an antrin flooer.

You mak girse grow fur baess
an coarn fur man ta use
so he can grow his crops
an mak bread ta gae him strent.

Da haands at med da sye
an hed da vynd ta maa
wid tak da jug, warm fae me skurt:
da haands at riped
da pages o Aurelius forbye.

Hame is biggit on a steid o wisdom.
Whar der is knowledge
da rooms is weel plenished.

Foonded in a laand
at nivver sklent tinkin
fae döin: dat saa wisdom
i da wark o haands.

(from Psalm 126 v 6; Song of Songs 2 v 12;
Psalm 104 v 14, 15; Proverbs 24 v 3)

---

strynd: *inherited trait*; dis: *this*; stricks: *strikes*; lem: *earthenware*; benkled: *bent*; faider: *father*; yerd: *enclosed field*; rowed: *rolled*; cloot: *cloth*; dem: *them*; at: *that*; gowled: *cried*; dey: *they*; gud: *went*; Kloss: *steep hill* ; doon'oose: *lower part of village*; doos: *pigeons*; een: *eyes*; sye: *scythe*; coarn: *oats*; swaars: *swathes cut by scythe*; stoor: *dust*; reeselled: *rummaged noisily*; truckin: *trampling*; ruckly: *uneven*; strae: *straw (stubble)*; antrin: *occasional*; flooer: *flower*; girse: *grass*; baess: *cattle*; strent: *strength*; vynd: *particular skill*; maa: *to reap*; skurt: *the bosom within the folded arms*; riped: *harvested*; biggit: *built*; steid: *foundation*; plenished: *fitted out*; sklent: *tore*; tinkin: *thinking*; döin: *doing*; dat: *that*; saa: *saw.*

35

There was no choice in footwear:
Clark's sandals, brown and roomy,
crepe rubber soles, T-strap, a buckle;
gloomy brown, with broad round toes
unchanging, indestructible.
Passed down through families,
across cousins. While we grew
and changed, they stayed
immutably the same.

Mother said
let your toes spread, little girl;
don't let them bunch. Let them expand
into this brown roundness.
Don't scrunch them up.
That way you'll have nice feet
when you grow up, no bunions.
And no, you needn't stamp your foot:
those golden shoes are not for school.
They're just for parties.
Once a year? Yes,
and don't screw up your face
my dear. And don't forget
the little Chinese girl
and what her mummy would have said.

I am cruel to be kind to you,
my toddler. I cannot shun
the evil hour a moment more.
When you are big, you'll thank me
that your feet are small.
In tiny golden slippers
your feet will be a sign of beauty.
I have to bend your toes like this,
bandage them tightly; put a stone
on top of them when you're asleep.
I have to break your bones, your will,
my little girl. Your will
is in your feet. Your beauty too.
If your feet can fit
these three inch slippers
you'll be subservient
to a wealthy husband.
If not, you'll be the servant
of a poor man, or no man at all.
I feel each breaking bone
as if it were my own.

So, my dear, think how fortunate you are
to feel that roominess, that leather strong.
Now buckle up your sandals, run along.

Cloistered in the infant room
we added up our certainty
and sums with plastic counters;
chanted our sounds as sonorously
as monks. On the wallchart
their novice shapes resounded
from the round 'a' of apple
to the tight, hard 'd' of drum.
We read, with hallowed focus
our first great chapter
of the 'Radiant Way':
"Ann can sing. Pat can sing.
Sing to Pat, mother."
We lined up to read, knew
the drill: the thrill of reaching
the top, the chill of faltering.
Down to the bottom of the line.
And the fine mystery of spelling:
to cipher and decipher words like
who and lamb, knife and gnome,
a penance of silent sounds.

Then it was writing. Miss Pole's
perfection on the blackboard.
She'd loop the l's and y's:
master choreographer of chalk.
Touching some lines, approaching
others; transforming qu's s to Q's
and t's to T's with ease. We'd copy
her movements, her sweep: follow,
heavy-footed, fumbling between lines,
filling pages with unholy rhymes.

Idder times

*Dey laid a foond for
generations still ta come,
layer on layer, beddin
planes o continuity.*

The outsiders

Dis muckle ston was riven fae some deep fiord side,
shakken oot o slumber lang sin syne. Hit lies
at Aness noo, ice-stivvened stranger, marking
glacial time; a grit galdery o quartz
herder an whiter is da ice at kyerried hit.
Hit cam afore da brochs or böds were built.
Picts wid a watched da dimriv splinter owre hit;
waeved tales and foys aroond hit's mystery;
weighed hit wi da mön, an tides an starns.
Maraudin Vikings could a coonted kin wi hit
takkin Helliness afore dem, namin is dey gud:
Fladdabister *'ferm on da flat laand'*; Okraquoy
'coarn growin apo scattald'. Dey settled aawye:
laid keels at Skibhul, keepit watch fae dere
apö Aid voe, lived oot der peerie saga.

An generations o udallers, der heirs, wir forbears
most a windered whit po'er, whit rage hed balled
dis faersome ston. Dem at brook oot laand,
built an taekit doon da years at Aness, dey böst
a sought some meaning fur hit's being dere.
Dey laid a foond for generations still ta come,
layer on layer, beddin planes o continuity.

An still we wander, come an geng
muv'd bi forces oot a wir control,
fin wirsels lodged in uncan pairts.
Da ooter layers, dey bruckle
peerie-wyes: wear doon, roond aff;
but no da inner places o da haert.

Sir William Armstrong, inventor
and Victorian philanthropist,
I tiptoe round your country house
stop respectfully at cord barriers.

I pass the fine statue on the stair
before I realise she's there, lifesize:
the handsome black girl in bronze.

Each room excels in harmony.
The 'Boudoir': now who could live
in such proportion, measured taste?
I almost long for something which looks
unmatched or out of place.

Here and there the walls are hung
with framed certificates, distinctions,
decorations and citations.
Photos show impressive guests:
The Prince of Wales,
The Crown Prince of Japan.

Everywhere are signs of your quick mind
and your inventiveness. Even in the kitchen
your designs made light of heavy jobs.
Each little inefficiency sparked off invention:
lifts and spits and water systems;

And at work, your designs progressed
from cranes and dock gates to artillery
and warships. Chains were slipped at Elswick
almost monthly from your Tyne-built ships.
Pride of the North-east they were:
sought by the world's navies. It's said
you rivalled even Krupp in ironclads.

And in the Civil War, Confederate
and Union gunned each other down
with your fine weaponry.   The profits paid
the architect, art-dealer, landscape-gardener,
portrait painter, taxidermist – quite the best –
the butterfly collector. They paid
for your enlightenment, your philanthropy.

They paid too for that residual pleasure:
that you would be remembered,
that people would contemplate
your brilliance and acquisitions.
Even the model warships are works of art.
The guns look almost decorative
like mouldings round the boudoir.

On the way out the beauty of your bronze
charms once again. This time I look more closely.
She is called "The Slave Girl". Only now I see
the well-wrought shackles on her wrists.
Her mien disarms.

Lunna, Shetland, c 1870

You say wir in debt
but I tell you, maister,
A'm no aksin fur mair is wir share.
You hae wis in troke,
me man haulin your tows
apö da far haaf, an me
seekin a paek o mel.

You can send me awa empty-handed
kennin wir laand is bön taen,
an park lambs is glunshin
whar wir baess wir wint ta be?

You ken fine when his boat
roonds da Lunna Holm
your beach'll be smored
in fat tusk an cod
while wir black fantin,
skeekin apon a sparl.

Heth! Let me tell you, maister,
whit Amos hed ta say
tae da hoose o Israel.
Da hill-grind is keepit da poor oota-daeks
awa fae der richt-fu laand.

Fur as muckle is your truckin is apö poor fock
an you tak fae dem a hirdin o bere,
da fine haa hooses at you built'll be vod.
Let judgement fill lik a gyill
an richt-daelin rin doon is a lipperin burn.
Sorro apö dem whase beds is weel plenished
at lie der lent apö saft restin-shairs,
an aet da lambs aff o da toons
an da quaigs oot o da byre.

Dem at said "Whan will da new mön be gien,
sae we can swick da ill-aff, buy dem fur siller,
an da pör-aamos fur a pair o shön
ya, an sell da oot-waelins o der aets?"

I tell you, maister, you can keep your mel,
fur da wye o da wicked sal perish
an der foy'll come tae an end.

(from Amos chapters 5 - 8; Psalm 1 v 6)

---

wir: *we are* ; aksin: *asking*; tows: *long hand-lines*; da: *the*; far haaf: *deep sea fishing grounds*;
paek: *small quantity*; mel: *oatmeal*; bön: *been*; glunshin: *swallowing greedily*; baess: *cattle*;
smored: *smothered*; tusk: *type of cod*; skeekin: *using sparingly*; sparl: *oat-stuffed intestine*;
Heth! *mild oath*; hill grind: *gate separating enclosed land from common hill land*; oota-daeks:
outside the hill dyke; truckin: *treading*; apö: *upon*; fock: *folk*; dem: *them*; hirdin: *harvest*;
haa: *laird's house*; vod: *unoccupied*; gyill: *head of valley*; is: *as*; lipperin: *overflowing*; weel
plenished: *well finished*; lie der lent: *lie, stretched out*; restin-shair: *long wooden seat with
arms*; aet: *eat*; toons: *arable strips*; quaigs: *heifers*; mön: *moon*; gien: *gone*; sae: *so*; swick:
cheat; ill-aff: *poor*; pör-aamos: *frail*; shön: *shoes*; oot-waelins: *leavings*; der: *their*; aets:
oats; wye: *way*; sal: *shall*; foy: *feast, party*.

Fedaland c 1887

Dis is wir hidmost simmer here at Fedaland.
Twal ton a olicks fur a saison's wark:
spleet eence apö da beach ta dry, but spleet
again bi da swing o da bismar's reckonin.

I sall miss da simmers on da outer rim; da bluntin
wind at lifts da sail, keeps wirds clos ta her breest.
An A'll miss da tilfer underfit, da gunwale's tilt,
relief when da green heicht o Fedaland comes near.

Foo fine hit wis apön a simmer's nicht, ta lay
da boat aff fae da aester ayre; ta sit
on da briggistane, broch at wir backs;
let faa da faer, recount da bravery.

I sall miss da beach at sheens lik mackreel scales,
da spreadin sillerweed, ticht glims o gowld;
tirricks liftin in a tirse, scarfs swaapin on da craigs
an weel kent stacks an taings an peerie gyos.

But A'll no miss da factor's graspin haand,
his tongue sharp is da horn aff da waster ayre; nor
da tocht at der's naethin ta shaa fur a saison's strug,
naethin ta fill a winter press. Na, far mair

I sall miss da sicht o a ranksman at da haaf;
a glisk o licht on his sail is we rin for hom,
reefed in, ridin da vaelensi – no aert-fast – seekin
a noost at da nort end o a nordern laand.

---

dis: *this*; wir: *our*; hidmost: *final*; twal: *twelve*; olicks: *young ling*; spleet: *split*; eence: *once*;
apö, apön: *on*; da: *the*; ta: *to*; bi: *by*; bismar: *wooden beam used for weighing goods*; sall:
shall; at: *that*; wirds: *words*; clos: *close*; tilfer: *floor plank in a boat*; foo: *how*; hit: *it*; wis:
was; aff: *off*; aester: *lying towards the east*; briggistane: *path of flat stones laid in front of
house*; mackreel: *mackerel*; sillerweed: *silverweed*; glim: *gleam*; gowld: *gold*; tirricks: *arctic
tern*; tirse: *temper, agitation*; scarfs: *shags*; swaapin: *beating their wings*; craigs: *flat rocks by
the shore*; taings: *flat promentaries*; peerie: *little*; gyo: *deep, narrow inlet*; no: *not*; horn:
rocky stack shaped like a horn; waster: *lying towards the west*; tocht: *thought*; at: *that*; shaa:
show; strug: *hard work*; ranksman: *one of two boats which fished in pairs for mutual aid*;
haaf: *deep sea fishing grounds*; glisk: *glimpse*; vaelensi: *violent gale*; aert-fast: *fixed firmly in
the ground*; noost: *hollow at edge of beach where boat is drawn up for safety*.

In Norrawa we had a dish o rømegrut
ta mark midsimmer: sweet mylk an bleddick
cookit tae a gruel. You supped again
your boyhood: aye myl-gruel in Vidlin

at johnsmas time: a treed spun
owre a thoosand simmer seas, at we,
wan generation, hed riven in favour
o low fat fromage frais.

You telt o johnsmas fires: emmers
o Viking taands at burned
on ness an taing, an still burn ta dis day
in Norrawa, atween fiords.

You minded stories tö o Dutchies
an der johnsmas foy in Lerwick,
da hidmost day afore dey set der sail
ta follow shoals o simmer herrin;

an hearin o da gig at cam at johnsmas
fur da gutters. Bi da saison's end
dey'd hae penga i der peenies, a string
o jet black beads, a laad, a haert-stane.

Neest johnsmas we'll mak fine gruel
wi crème fraîche fae Isigny.
Wi a spön o honey hit'll mak a feast
fur John da Baptist's day.

Wir peerie foy'll see nae Dutchies
dirlin doon da street; nae gig
o gaffin lasses, arles lang ta'en
afore da aggle o da creel.

We'll no let johnsmas come an geng
ithoot a bonfire, an wir myl-gruel.
We'll celebrate da langest day, an trivvel
till we fin dat tinnest treed ta tie secure.

---

myl-gruel: *oatmeal porridge made with milk instead of water*; da: *the*; Norrawa: *Norway*;
rømegrut: *midsummer porridge-type treat made with sour cream*; sweet mylk: *fresh milk*;
bleddick: *buttermilk*; tae, ta: *to*; johnsmas: *June 24th*; treed: *thread*; owre: *over*; wan: *one*;
hed: *had*; riven: *torn*; telt: *told*; emmers: *embers*; taand: *a firebrand of peat*; at: *that*; taing:
flat promentary; dis: *this*; atween: *between*; minded: *remembered*; tö: *too*; der: *their*;
johnsmas foy: *the celebration which was held by Dutch fishermen in Lerwick before the herring
season began*; hidmost: *final*; afore: *before*; dey: *they*; cam: *came*; bi: *by*; penga: *money*;
i: *in*; laad: *boyfriend*; haert-stane: *hearth*; neest: *next*; spön: *spoon*; wir: *our*; peerie: *little*;
dirlin: *vibrating (clogs)*; gaffin: *laughing*; arles ta'en: *having made a commitment to a season's
work for which a retainer fee was paid*; aggle: *mess*; geng: *go*; ithoot: *without*; trivvel: *grope*;
fin: *find*; dat: *that*; tinnest: *thinnest*.

I drive da oil road nort fae Gott:
October hills ir cled in moorit,
in dowed pinks an gowld;
paet hags in Shetland black
drittle doon da broos
lik slippit loops.

I stop at Sandwater; catch colours
i da loch; catch sicht o generations gien.
A mird o fock on aa gaets tae da roup here:
sheep ca'ad fae Kergord early
owre da Lamba Skord; dugs rinnin, dippin
- twa lambs fur sixpence -

a platsh o filsket quaigs
fae Lunna Ness an Voe.
An early rise, a lang day gyaan,
a langer traivel hame.
Mirknen lowsed stories o fock spirited awa;
o trows' hadds i da hills
an dark Pettawater foo o gluffs.

I drive da empty road
- lang Kames ta aest an wast -
followin da gaet o ice. Ten thoosand year
o moor cled hills an deepenin paet sin syne.
I strip dem bare. Grit judderin fingers cloorin
at da solid haert, skrovvelin tae da suddert, rivin
der gaets trowe Pettadal ta Strom;
trowe Kergord, on ta Weisdale, Hoy;
an Laxfirt trowe ta Scallawa an on.
Dan slow uplowsin: grit poans o ice
owre aathin, sturkenin, slowin;
water aawye, an bare hills clerted
wi da bruckled lod.

I drive da oil rod nort ta Sullom Voe,
seekin lik da first bird
muvin nort wi warmin air.
A fast road noo, barely a bend:
yet just a peerie scam apö dis aert.

Whin fock look back millenia ahead
will dey see treeds fae dis short century
whase years saw mair is colours change?

---

aa: *all;* da: *the;* cled: *clad;* moorit: *natural brown;* Shetland black: *dark brown;* drittle: *to walk aimlessly;* broos: *brow of hill;* loops: *stitches;* gien: *gone;* mird: *throng;* fock: *folk;* gaets: *paths;* roup: *auction sale;* ca'ad: *driven, herded;* platsh: *from verb to walk heavily through wet ground;* filsket: *frisky;* quaigs: *heifers;* gyaan: *going;* traivel: *walk;* mirknen: *twilight;* lowsed: *loosened;* trows' hadds: *habitations of trolls;* foo: *full;* gluffs: *frights;* sin syne: *since then;* grit: *large;* cloorin: *clawing;* skrovvelin: *groping;* suddert: *southwards;* rivin: *tearing;* dan: *then;* uplowsin: *thaw;* poans: *layers (usually of turf);* aathin: *everything;* sturkenin: *unable to move (coagulating);* aawye: *everywhere;* clerted: *besmeared;* bruckled: *fragmented;* lod: *load;* muvin: *moving;* noo: *now;* peerie: *small;* scam: *blemish;* apö: *upon;* dis: *this;* treeds: *threads.*

Madonna della Candelatta:
can this be me, so blonde and perfect
this sad, crowned figure?
Perhaps Crivelli's model was his mistress
the one he went to jail for.
This sheening queenliness
this miserable babe: *henceforth*
all generations shall call me blessed.
For He that is mighty hath done
to me great things.
Whose are the words, *Magnificat?*
Who put these learned phrases in my mouth:
the strident calls through centuries
of prophets, priests and kings?

Raphael's Madonna of the Goldfinch:
I could wish to emulate this pious beauty
this sensuality: humility of downcast eye
for He hath regarded the low estate
of his handmaiden.
The clothes at least look travel worn,
but did I plait a head of golden hair
in courtly style?
Where is my Jewishness?

Carracci's drawing has me lithe
and lovely, the baby ringed around
by brawny shepherds:
men who have lifted sheep, chased wolves away.
He hath exalted them of low degree.
He hath scattered the proud in the imagination
of their hearts.

Van Honthorst paints me pleased
and plain and motherly; a habitation for mankind.
There's happiness in all the faces.
My soul doth magnify the Lord.

In Van der Werff's depiction
I'm uninvolved; a saintly pawn.
His cherubs may be fine
and that fashionable hat
presumably mine. But he has painted me
as cold, although I'm bathed in light;
cold as that mercy which depends on fear
from generation to generation.
Those hands, like a princess
delicate and pale.
Where are the hands that tilled and reaped
the roughened skin that held salvation?
Where is perplexity and tiredness?
Where is the fear?

Cromarty, 1920s

I carry our baited lines to the shore,
lift you on my back at the water's edge,
wade with you to the boat. It steadies me:
the keel, half-grounded, half afloat.
Your feet will be dry when you raise the sail.
There is nothing frail left in me:
though salt stings, it heals.

I walk up the beach, unsteady in my lightness:
only the child to carry now. The season
will be through before the birth.
He will be rocked by generations.
I am proud that only I will lift you.

Your danger, my trachle, like anchors:
deep holds of our days and nights.

I run to the beach when I see your sail.
You trail a rope as you leap, first ashore,
wet to the waist. We get our portion.
You lift a scoo to my shoulder;

I wrap fish in a hoarse song of selling;
move between houses on my way,
while you unfurl, soothe your body at my fire.

Our bed is the slackening curl of the tide:
at your side I drift to a new day.

scoo: *basket for fish.*

Survival tactics

Out there are days:
tomorrows whose weights
are beyond lifting.

Earth has taken you:
the wind has shaken your rugs,
beaten the dust of death from them.
Symbols of your illness
have been set alight.
They are ash now.
Earth, wind and fire
have had their turn, conspired
against death's listlessness.
They have picked it clean,
linked arms with it,
are implicated in its sense
of ending.

We have hunched long
in quiet rooms. Let us now run
in open spaces, stretch beyond
dark traces of mortality.
Let us tread barefoot
on beach stones, scrunch
tidelines noisily, watch
the sea rinse every crevice,
roll the edges of death back
with every wave rush.

This is ritual cleansing,
intuitive remnant
of Euphrates, Ganges.

Somewhere,
between conscious and subconscious, lurk
labyrinths: spaces of no fixed dimension.
They hold distillations of all our battles,
lost or won, all skirmishes. Lift the stoppers
and each gives off its bilious vapours,
more noxious than the day they swept in,
all huffs and puffs, resentments, hurts.

Some seep gradually to inner rooms,
to long term storage, archived
beyond the pale of graciousness:
unholy of unforgiving holies.
Each leaves a trail, a lingering
odour, carefully cross-referenced
to aid retrieval in extremis.

Beware, their half-life
may yet outlive us.

Tap the barometer
and the needle falls.

What is more absurd:
a calm voice intoning
a shipping forecast;
sea areas listed
in prescribed order,
force 10, veering,
imminent? Or gales

of bleak unreason
thrown up from nowhere:
threats which life's ballast
cannot weigh against?

Instinct suggests
search for its eye
bend to its rage
till it dissipates.

It takes fearlessness
to steer into the wind;
to take the waves head on.

You have retreated
into the singularity:
imploded into a deluge
of inexistence.

Out there are days:
tomorrows whose weights
are beyond lifting. Somehow
even yesterdays are relative,
have lost their focus, their reality.
There is only an interminable now.

The catalogue of things we do
looks long and burdensome.
There's little point. You're through

with words picked up and strung in sentences.
They cannot express this dearth of future.
They are too heavy anyhow:
heavier than silence. But now

at last your voice is lighter,
lighter than for months.
You lift the smallest skylight on your world:
ask me how I am, and when I'll come.

I sense the dove you sent out
has brought back hope, a slip of greening.
And that you've held the singularity
in your sights, and blown it free,
dared to stare future in the face
and once again believe.

I am here to rid myself of shadows.
This is the spot mapped
indelibly on my mind.
After decades I have come back.

That day
walking by this loch
warm with my mother
we feed swans.
I splash a stone: it circles
my aura of safety, blends
rim with centre. I stretch
the invisible circumference,
probe its instancy,
its innocent limits
of water, birds and stone.

I am here now
at this most terrible spot
where he approached
where memory resonates
in cold, decreasing rings;
reiterates its fear.
Though meanings were unclear
there was something shameful,
something which would stain
all my childhood roaming.

The chill still prickles on my neck
and even now, there is relief
returning home.

Psychologists can prove
that images come at us upside
down, and that we've learned
to turn them right way up;

and scientists hold
that in this infinitude
which is the universe
there is no fixed point.
Earth tilts around a sun star
which in turn pulls all its planets
round the Milky Way.
At half-a-million miles per hour
it takes 500 times as many years
to birl right round; and even then
the starting point has shifted.
All is on the move, expanding, relative,
held in the tenuous grip of gravity.

Unshaken by this tyranny
that holds the heavens
I look out on my garden, stare
at the huge stability of trees
rooted downwards, their light leaves
right way up to the sun,
finding gravity a pushover,
the wind kittenish.

From the windowsill, the stillest
of grey squirrels eyes me, anticipates
a second helping. It is her season
of making ready, of waiting.

Our caterpillar in the sweetie jar
has woven a cocoon. It is brown
with round ends, precision engineering.
He measures metamorphosis in months.

In a basin, orphaned tadpoles lie quiet,
unmoved by night or day, hung
between jellied egg and gulping frog-ness.
They wait weeks for legs and lungs.

Our grey cat brushes past, spelling
tea-time round my legs.
His stomach is his clock, accurate
as the quartz of his eye. He is fed

whenever he comes, spoiled creature.
But for me, I stalk time, hunt it
through the sun's clear demarcations;
pounce on the season, the moment.

Louvre, D'Orsay, Beaubourg:
such gendered creativity begs questions.
I need blank space to recollect
the undone art, the missing canvases.

Was paint too masculine, too louche
a medium for women? Did it lack
a homely function; require
uninterrupted hours, demand
obsession; jealously devour a passion?

You had your models sit stock still,
until the image had been captured;
then hung them, constrained
in frames, on walls of galleries.

Mona Lisa, you still can pull a crowd,
virgin, nymph and goddess all in one.
Would that you could run amok,
shake off that comeliness, strike out
and daub some great graffiti, splash
paint across sequestered centuries;
tell it like it was, and is, and will be.

But wait,
before you slip your painted shackles,
smile for the young man watching you.
He has a baby on his back.

Poems for bairns

"Daa, I wid lik ta see dis trows
at mak wir wirld sae fine."
"Na, jewel, dey'r braaly blate
hit seems, an canna
see a stime."

da: *the*; Yöl: *Christmas*; Santy: *Santa Claus*; trowe: *through*; lambie-hoose: *low thatched building used to shelter lambs or weak sheep*; whar: *where*; neebin: *nodding with sleep*; his lane: *on his own*; dy: *your (familiar)*; een: *one*; is snappered: *has stumbled*; med: *made, reached*; flee: *fly*; telt: *told*; dat: *that*; clushit: *very clumsy*; crabbit: *bad tempered*; nivver leet: *never heed*; dee: *you (familiar)*; dis: *this*; yokit: *yoked*; bend: *harness of peat-pony*; hirplin: *limping*; lock: *a large amount*; dön: *done*; wis: *us*; sigg im!: *an exclamation to incite chase*; aa: *all*; po'er: *power*; dey: *they*; is: *as*; slippit: *slipped*; tanks: *thanks*; peerie: *little*; apö: *on*; wir: *were*; blyde: *glad*; tocht: *thought*; lift: *heavens, sky*.

Bairn rhyme

Santy cam in trowe da lambie-hoose door
whar Magnus wis neebin his lane.
"A'm needin dy help, fur een o my deer
is snappered an med himsel lame."

"But I canna flee" said Magnus, "in truth
A'm telt dat A'm clushit an crabbit."
"Nivver leet" said auld Santy, "I need dee da nicht
fur dis bag is sae heavy an stappit."

So he yokit up Magnus wi bend an wi bells
an left da hirplin deer bedded;
"Noo tak a deep breath an wir up i da cloods!"
Dey lifted aff just is he said hit.

"We'll hae ta hurry, der's a lock ta be dön,
a time zone ta cross every hour
or da sunrise'll catch wis oot i da aest
sae 'sigg im!' Use aa dy po'er."

Dey med every hoose bi da end o da nicht
is da wirld turned roond tae da sun;
dan dey slippit aff Magnus, wi tanks an a wave
at da lambie-hoose whar dey'd begun.

Is peerie bairns waakened apö da Yöl moarn
dey wir blyde ta see Santy hed been.
Little tocht dey a pony hed sped trowe da lift.
Ta Magnus hit seemed lik a draem.

Bairn rhyme

"Tammy Noddy's late da nicht.
Get dee tae dy bed
or du'll be raamised aa da moarn.
White whissin lik I said!"

"Daa, foo's a möldie-blett med
wi naethin growin dere?
I tink hit's whaar a UFO
scoodered da heogan bare."

"Na, naethin supernatural:
hit's just whaar peerie trows
decided dey wid hae a foy,
an cleared da hedder-kowes."

"An faider, whit's yon muckle sten
at staands apö da knowe?
Did ice raft hit fae Norrawa
an drap him when hit towed?"

"Na, naethin quite sae fanciful:
hit's whaar trows buried kings,
laid up der guddicks, sang der rhymes,
an danced aroond in rings."

"An whit is aa yon paet-hags, daa;
foo come dey cam ta be?
Ir dey da gaets whaar trowie fock
wid rin an hae a spree?"

"Na, far mair doon ta aert, boy,
hit's der peerie paety banks:
tushkers trivvellin i da mirk
med aa yon skew-wheef stanks."

"Daa, I wid lik ta see dis trows
at mak wir wirld sae fine."
"Na, jewel, dey'r braaly blate, hit seems,
an canna see a stime.

Dey'r only oot whin da mön is foo
an du's tuckit up at nicht.
Sae geng dee wis ta bed, me boy,
an mind an slock dy licht."

---

trow: *troll, mischievous fairy*; Tammy Noddy: *a child's name for sleep*; da nicht: *tonight*; dee:
you (familiar); dy: *your (familiar)*; du: *you (familiar)*; raamised: *peevish through lack of
sleep*; aa: *all*; da moarn: *tomorrow*; white: *stop, cease*; whissin: *questioning*; daa, faider:
father; foo: *how*; möldie blett: *bare patch of hill pasture from which peat mould was gathered
for bedding cattle*; med: *made*; dere: *there*; tink: *think*; hit: *it*; scoodered: *scorched*; heogan:
common hill land; peerie: *little*; dey: *they*; wid: *would*; foy: *celebration, party*; hedder-
kowes: *bushy heather plants*; at: *that*; apö: *on*; Norrowa: *Norway*; towed: *thawed*; whaar:
where; laid up der guddicks: *asked their riddles*; yon: *those*; ir: *are*; gaets: *paths*;
spree: *jollification*; aert: *earth*; der: *their*; tushkers: *peat-cutting spades*; trivvelin: *groping*;
i: *in*; mirk: *darkness*; skew-wheef: *squint*; stank: *ditch*; dis: *this, these*; wir: *our*; jewel:
term of endearment; braaly: *fairly*; blate: *shy, timid*; canna: *can not*; stime: *a faint trace of
anything*; mön: *moon*; foo: *full*; geng dee wis: *go*; mind: *remember*; slock: *extinguish*.

Foo ta keep sheep ithoot a ram or a dug

Wir first yowe cam fae Auntie Bab -
ca'ad eftir her. Dan twartree mair
we named bi whaar dey cam fae.

Dat almark Sannis wis a trooker;
Baaka, biddable an blate;
an John Tamson, a traan gimmer.

Wi nae ram, dey gud fur a "brack"
afore winter set in; tippit hame
wi paint apö der backs.

I da winter, eftir scöl, we brought
yowe-nuts, an a shöl o peerie tatties.
Dey lippened wis, cam rinnin.

Lambs drappit i da cold voar,
shön warmed wi a midder's lickin
an her mylk, tails spricklin.

Da caa, an nae dug but wis ta rin.
Whit a dereeshion! Aa but dere,
dan aff again, Göd kens whaar.

I da crö at last, ready fur rooin.
We pooed der oo aff, creeshy an warm.
Dan fled fae da "sortin": for sic a nyaarm.

I da hairst time, a caa fur dippin:
wan bi wan i da trough, richt under,
we were faered dey wid smore.

An dan da pairtin, lambs fae midders:
dey gret aa day an da neest een.
A black day hit wis, but blacker

da final ontack: da roup or da tully.
Facts o life at we learned,
at da fleece underfit nivver saafened.

Alzheimer
sequence

I sing for you,
and wonderfully you join in,
add harmony.

You cannot recognise me now
but welcome me, companion for a time.
I walk the wilderness with you,
search like the wandering Israelites.
Will there be answers in this secret place
of thunder, of murmurings?

The wilderness within you has been stripped.
Only the grain is left.   And yet, despite erosion,
much remains to cross the chasms;
a touch, a smile. Your muddled words
are full of thoughtfulness.

I sing for you, and wonderfully
you join in, add harmony.

Then shall the tongue of the dumb sing:
for in the wilderness shall waters break out,
streams in the desert.

I feel as Moses must have felt
striking the rock.

(from Psalm 81, v7; Exodus 17; Isaiah 35, v6)

I have seen angels:
they wear uniform
and tend the senile
in locked wards.

Their messages are simple.
'Here's your cocoa, George;
no, try the other hand.
I'll hold it for you.'

No light attends their ministerings
as they console
the mad and mindless,
search out the dignity
that's dribbling, stumbling,
shouting.

'No, Betty, keep your tights on.
It's not quite bedtime yet, love,
won't be long.'

They smooth the edges
bear the unbearable,
stare into the face
of their own frailness,
contain the furies
till they ease
in death's slip stream.

I have seen angels:
they partner fear,
dance with our demons,
tend the senile
in locked wards.

After the food, the picnic extends
into rounders, face-painting,
parachute games.

You are parked at the edge,
rug round your angular frame.
Two little girls sit with you.
Their legs dangle.

In this snug circle of prattle
they steal your label of senility:
their words and yours hold
no more than the moment

make no demands.
But your glow shows
you still know companionship,
the art of being.

On this warm day
each of you almost masters
the lesser art of the ice cream cone.
Seeing it daubed on your nose,
one of them laughs,
points to the place. You smile
with your eyes, lean
contentedly, unsurprised

by the huge butterfly painted
on her perfect face.

I sing and you join in.
Your voice has timbre, steadiness.
You keep the tune, find old bass notes,
sense your success.

But this last movement could be called
discordant: a fractured melody.
The great crescendos of your days of words
are only echoes. Among
these restless souls you're back
at the beginning, tuning up.

Words are scarcer now.
And when they come
your tone unlocks their mystery:
distress or happiness.

But saying things your special way,
with music in your eyes, it seems
you still defy cacophony.

From your cot you smile as I approach,
child man, spirit man. I drop
the cot-side, stroke your frail head.
Your word today is 'happy'. I take
your beaming gift.

From a curtained bed
loud curses cut the ward.
You sense indignity; anger
at that tender nursing
even babies kick against.

You find another word: 'blessings'.
It leaps the barricades, invades
his territory, his space of suffering.
His fearfulness is staunched
by this strange salvo.

Your rare words heal like balsam:
as gifts, transform.

for Alex and Zena

You hover at the door as I arrive.
The wave suggests you recognise me.
Not that it matters. Ward keys
are turned. I breach the glass edge
of your world, scale the precipice.
Today it's you who greets me with a kiss.
That's a surprise: the word has gone,
but not the pleasure or the sign.

You speak of Zena many times today.
"Zena, dear": two words welded
in your deepest mind. "She's coming
soon" I say. You're in the mood
to talk. She'll be so pleased to know
you said her name. I try to hold
your phrases in my head to tell her.
"It's very lovely" and "I've no doubt
at all of that" and, true to character,
"We're very fortunate."

This universe of yours is reeling
with abandoned souls, littered
with their verbal debris.
But out and in among,
you still can say it all.
Your undiminished song
and all the wordless spaces held
between you, just like you say,
are "good and strong."

As you drift gently from us there will be
spring garlands, a descant of song.
In our hearts we will dance long for you,
round all imaginable maypoles;
through breath of blossom, as it falls
wind-sifted. For you are lightness, essence;
a still smiling presence ahead of us,
for whom the burden of time has lifted.

Postscript

*You straddle our land
with a conclusion
of cathedrals.*

We are a tented people
murmuring against ourselves,
lifting stones for words
and building narrow chapels.

Your poems house us
with artless ease
and feed us manna
a never-ending feast.

You straddle our land
with a conclusion
of cathedrals.